CPSIA information can be obtained
at www.ICGtesting.com
Printed in the USA
LVHW031342151019
634130LV00009B/2800/P